108

"Natural" Alternatives to Antidepressants

St. John's Wort, Kava Kava, and Others

ANTIDEPRESSANTS

"Natural" Alternatives to Antidepressants

St. John's Wort, Kava Kava, and Others

by Kenneth McIntosh

Mason Crest Publishers

Philadelphia

Mason Crest Publishers Inc.
370 Reed Road
Broomall, Pennsylvania 19008
(866) MCP-BOOK (toll free)

First printing
1 2 3 4 5 6 7 8 9 10
        Library of Congress Cataloging-in-Publication Data

McIntosh, Kenneth, 1959-
  Natural alternatives to antidepressants : St. John's wort, kava kava, and
others / by Kenneth McIntosh.
      p. cm.
  Includes bibliographical references and index.
  ISBN 1-4222-0105-8   ISBN (series) 1-4222-0094-9
  1. Depression, Mental—Alternative treatment—Juvenile literature.
I. Title.
  RC537.M3946 2007
  616.85'2706—dc22
                              2006016123

Interior design by MK Bassett-Harvey.
Interiors produced by Harding House Publishing Service, Inc.
www.hardinghousepages.com.
Cover design by Peter Culatta.
Printed in the Hashemite Kingdom of Jordan.

Contents

Introduction

by Andrew M. Kleiman, M.D.

From ancient Greece through the twenty-first century, the experience of sadness and depression is one of the many that define humanity. As long as human beings have felt emotions, they have endured depression. Experienced by people from every race, socioeconomic class, age group, and culture, depression is an emotional and physical experience that millions of people suffer each day. Despite being described in literature and music; examined by countless scientists, philosophers, and thinkers; and studied and treated for centuries, depression continues to remain as complex and mysterious as ever.

In today's Western culture, hearing about depression and treatments for depression is common. Adolescents in particular are bombarded with information, warnings, recommendations, and suggestions. It is critical that adolescents and young people have an understanding of depression and its impact on an individual's psychological and physical health, as well as the treatment options available to help those who suffer from depression.

Why? Because depression can lead to poor school performance, isolation from family and friends, alcohol and drug abuse, and even suicide. This doesn't have to be the case, since many useful and promising treatments exist to relieve the suffering of those with depression. Treatments for depression may also pose certain risks, however.

Since the beginning of civilization, people have been trying to alleviate the suffering of those with depression. Modern-day medicine and psychology have taken the understanding and treatment of depression to new heights. Despite their shortcomings, these treatments have helped millions and millions of people lead happier, more fulfilling and prosperous lives that would not be possible in generations past. These treatments, however, have their own risks, and for some people, may not be effective at all. Much work in neuroscience, medicine, and psychology needs to be done in the years to come.

Many adolescents experience depression, and this book series will help young people to recognize depression both in themselves and in those around them. It will give them the basic understanding of the history of depression and the various treatments that have been used to combat depression over the years. The books will also provide a basic scientific understanding of depression, and the many biological, psychological, and alternative treatments available to someone suffering from depression today.

Each person's brain and biology, life experiences, thoughts, and day-to-day situations are unique. Similarly, each individual experiences depression and sadness in a unique way. Each adolescent suffering from depression thus requires a distinct, individual treatment plan that best suits his or her needs. This series promises to be a vital resource for helping young people recognize and understand depression, and make informed and thoughtful decisions regarding treatment.

Chapter 1

Depression, Drugs, and Decisions

Hi Sis,

How are things at Berkeley? Are you holding up OK with your classes and your job? I sure miss seeing you at home. I know we always got into fights, but it isn't the same with my big sister gone!

Do you mind if I ask you for some advice? I figure with you going to medical school, you probably know a lot more about this than I do. I suppose I should be talking with Mom about this, but we aren't getting along real great, and it was always easier asking you about things.

Everyone feels tearful sometimes, but prolonged periods of sadness and crying could indicate a more serious depression.

I've been feeling really crappy lately. No, to be honest, I've been feeling this way for a long time. I've been feeling really sad, really down. Sometimes I have to cut out of class and go to the bathroom, where I just go in a stall and cry for a few minutes, and then I go back to class and keep going like nothing happened. At first, I thought I was down about Mom and Dad's divorce, but that was a year ago, and I don't really think that much about it. I don't know why I'm so down. I feel real tired, too—like no energy. I quit playing b-ball down at the park because I just don't feel like running up and down the court, and a lot of times I don't want to be with anyone. So I come home, do my homework, and go to sleep early.

I talked to our old neighbor Alyssa: she says I'm depressed, and I should get Mom to take me to the doctor for a prescription. She says she used to feel like I do, but now she has a prescription for Zoloft®, and she feels a lot better.

I wasn't looking forward to talking with Mom about this, but I was ready to do what Alyssa said; then yesterday I was hanging out with Malu (remember her? she's my friend that moved here from Hawaii). She was talking about how bad she used to feel all the time, and how she began practicing natural treatment for her depression. She takes something called St. John's wort, and she watches her diet, and she goes jogging every day, and she says she feels all better. Malu also had some scary stuff to say about the medicines doctors give you for depression—she says they're actually dangerous, and they can even make people suicidal.

So, now I'm confused—and I still feel like crap. I can't keep on going like this, but I don't know which way to go; if I tell Mom, she'll take me to a doctor's appointment right away, and she'll insist I take prescription meds, and I won't have any choice about it. Malu says I can do everything she does without a doctor, but it will take money and energy, and I really don't know much about it.

What should I do? It just totally stinks feeling this way, I have to do something. I'm confused. Thanks for letting me spill this on you, but I figure that's what big sisters are for, especially when they're at medical school.

—Krystal

Hey Krystal,

I'm so glad you told me about how you're feeling—I always want to know what's going on with my little sister! I could tell from your recent messages that you weren't feeling so great, but didn't realize you were so depressed. This sounds like serious stuff—if you're feeling this bad this long, it probably won't go away by itself, so I agree with both Alyssa and Malu: you should do something about the way you are feeling.

Should you go with natural or pharmaceutical treatments? I can't tell you what you should do just from reading your e-mail; and besides, I'm your big sis, not a psychologist! But I do have some advice. Go ahead and talk to Mom. Believe me, Krys, she loves us, and I think she'll do more good than harm in your situation. Ask Mom to check

Natural medicines are often made from plant extracts.

around and find a doctor who is willing to consider alternative treatments for depression. That way you have a no-lose situation; if you can find a good psychiatrist or doctor, he or she can help you decide which way is best for you.

I love you Krys, I miss you a lot, and I'll be sending good thoughts your way.

—Linda (Sis)

Depression: The Mind–Body Affliction

Everyone feels "blue" sometimes, but the word "depression" means more than just "feeling bad." Depression is a mood disorder that influences both mind and body, causing profound sadness and a decreased ability to experience pleasure. Depression influences the entire body, altering patterns of sleep, eating, concentration, and exercise. Depression isn't just one disease: in fact there are several forms of depressive disorders.

Causes of Depression

Even with all the scientific discoveries of recent decades, in the twenty-first century, experts still disagree as to causes of the illness. There are two major theories: ***psychosocial*** theories versus ***neurobiological*** theories. Psychosocial theories regard depression as mostly a behavioral and emotional problem, resulting from life experiences and situations. Contrasting with this view, neurobiological theories focus on

Types of Depression

- Major depressive disorder lasts for two weeks or more and involves a very low mood and lack of interest in pleasures.

- Dysthymia is usually less severe than major depressive disorder; however it tends to be longer lasting (chronic).

- Adjustment disorder with depressed mood (situational or reactive depression) is a reaction to bad events such as family problems, relationship problems, or natural disasters.

- Bipolar disorder (manic-depressive) is a mood disorder with a depressive component. It is characterized by changes in mood: from excited and energetic to depressed and desolate.

- Seasonal affective disorder (SAD) makes people feel unhappy during long, dark winters.

- Depression related to hormones affects a small percentage of women who suffer symptoms known as premenstrual dysphoric disorder (PMDD), an extreme form of mood changes associated with the more common premenstrual syndrome (PMS). Postpartum depression following childbirth might also be related to changes in female hormone levels.

the "hardware" of the mind and body; depression is viewed as genetic or physical in nature.

A majority of doctors and psychologists, however, agree that *both* mind and matter contribute to the causes of depression. Clinical psychologists Laura L. Smith and Charles H. Elliot say, "Most sophisticated experts in the field of depression know that a single, definitive cause of depression . . . likely will never be discovered."

Antidepressant Medications for Depression

The most commonly used prescription drugs for depression are SSRIs (selective serotonin reuptake inhibitors). These include brand name Paxil® (generic name paroxetine hydrochloride), Prozac® (fluoxetine hydrochloride), and Zoloft® (sertraline hydrochloride). Worldwide, more than 50 million people have taken Prozac, and millions more have taken other SSRIs.

Experts are uncertain exactly how these drugs work, but they have a general idea. Your brain contains approximately 100 billion **neurons** that control your actions, thoughts, and emotions. Serotonin is a chemical neurons use to communicate with each other, and SSRIs alter the amount of serotonin used by the neurons, hence altering moods.

Allegations Against Antidepressant Medications

There have been highly publicized charges that antidepressant medications may cause suicide, but such allegations remain

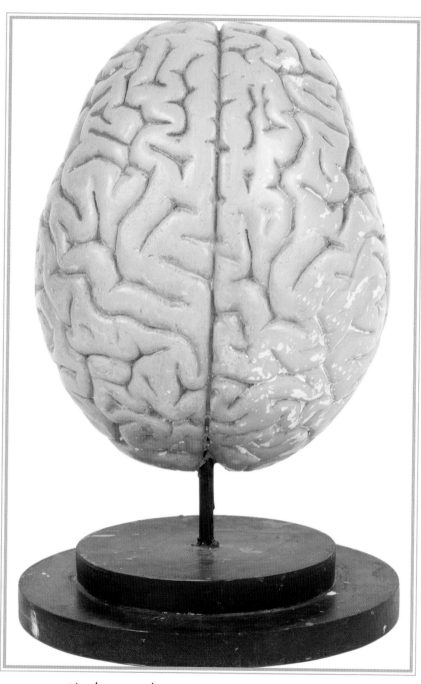

The human brain contains approximately
100 billion nerve cells.

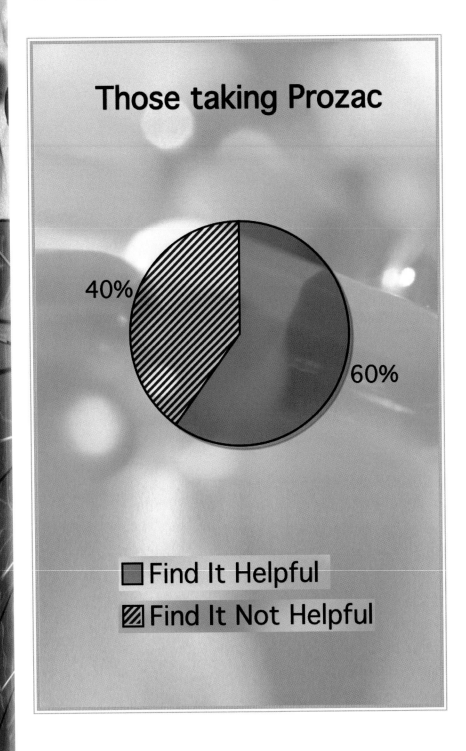

Those taking Prozac

40%

60%

☐ Find It Helpful

▨ Find It Not Helpful

and Name vs. Generic Name

king about psychiatric drugs can be confusing, because every drug
at least two names: its "generic name" and the "brand name" that the
armaceutical company uses to market the drug. Generic names come
m the drugs' chemical structure, while drug companies use brand
nes in order inspire public recognition and loyalty for their products.

unproven. As medicine reporter Denise Grady wrote in 1990,
"Given that 30,000 Americans a year were killing themselves
before Prozac came along, it may be hard to prove that patients became suicidal from Prozac and not from depression
itself." Studies show Prozac is helpful to approximately 60
percent of patients, and the number of patients who commit
suicide while on antidepressants is unfortunately the number
one would expect, even if the medications are effective. However, in July of 2005, the U.S. Food and Drug Administration
(FDA) issued a public health advisory stating "Adults whose
symptoms worsen while being treated with antidepressants,
including an increase in suicidal thinking or behavior, should
be evaluated by their health care professional."

In January of 2006, a pair of federally funded studies sup-
ported the safety of antidepressant medications. The first
study surveyed three thousand adults and found that half

experienced some improvement from major depression after taking antidepressant medications. The second study of 65,000 adults and teens affirmed that antidepressant medications lessened the likelihood of suicide in patients with depression. Most physicians and scientists regard today's prescription medications as safe and effective for treating depression, and antidepressant drugs are the most commonly prescribed remedies for mood disorders. Some doctors fear bad press about antidepressant medicines may prevent people with depression from taking drugs that could save them from suicide or other harmful actions.

Popularity of Natural and Alternative Treatments

Since so many people have fears and misgivings about pharmaceutical treatments for depression, it is not surprising that natural and alternative treatments are hugely popular. A survey reported in the February 2001 issue of the *American Journal of Psychiatry* found more than half of those surveyed with cases of major depression used alternative treatments such as herbs, spiritual healing, vitamins, and special diets; furthermore, the majority of these patients reported that alternative treatments were helpful.

What Does "Natural" Mean?

In books, magazines, and on the Internet, the terms "natural" or "alternative" are used very loosely when speaking of health treatments. Syd Baumel, author of *Dealing with*

Asian medical traditions offer many varieties of alternative treatments.

*Yoga is one of the many forms of alternative
treatments that are rooted in the East.*

Depression Naturally, defines natural treatments as "a very wide spectrum that excludes artificial/human-made drugs and includes such things as diet, exercise, meditation, psychotherapy, herbs, and preventative/therapeutic lifestyle changes." A similar term is alternative treatments, defined as "health-care practices considered outside the scope of conventional Western medicine" including **homeopathy**, yoga, **Qi gong**, **Reiki**, and other practices. Doctors Laura L. Smith and Charles H. Elliott explain:

> We consider treatments for depression to be alternative if they're either not widely accepted as effective by conventional mental health and medical professionals or if these professionals don't use treatments as first-choice approaches for most cases of major depression.

Natural medicines are an enormous industry, and a veritable ocean of Internet sites, books, and magazines advertise natural remedies. Many people who have suffered from depression say natural treatments freed them from the despair that formerly held them in its grip. Yet questions remain: are "natural" medicines necessarily "healthier," "better," or "safer" than over-the-counter or prescription drugs?

Chapter 2

Does "Natural" Mean "Better"?

Hi again Sis,

I appreciate your advice, but I'm still not sure I want to talk to Mom. She's so definite about things; I want to know what I think is right before talking to her. Malu sent me some links to sites about natural treatment for depression. There are so many choices and things I never even heard of: ginkgo biloba, St. John's wort, kava kava.

I noticed whatever I'm reading about, there seems to be someone on the site claiming what a miracle the treatment is, and how it helped him when nothing else did, and

Just because something is natural does not mean that it is safe. Wild mushrooms like this are natural—and poisonous!

yada-yada-yada. I guess I'm just cynical, but I have to wonder: if each of these is such a wonderful cure, how come so
many people are still depressed?

At the same time, I like that word "natural." I mean, who
wants to put something that's not natural in her body? And
the arguments for natural medicines sound good. Things
that nature made should work better in our systems than
something cooked up in a laboratory, right? And some of
these cures have been used for a long time before people
discovered modern science.

I know you already gave me advice, and I wish I could
just listen to it, but I'm afraid to do anything right now.
Could you give me some facts? Does "natural" necessarily mean "better," and are the prescription drugs really as
dangerous as they say?

Thanks for being patient with me. I really need to get
things sorted out!

—Krystal

Hi Krys,

"Does 'natural' always mean 'better'?" Not necessarily.
Some things that are 100 percent natural can kill you: for
example, some wild mushrooms are totally lethal—that's
why mushroom gatherers have to be very careful. I'm
not saying natural treatments are necessarily dangerous,
just that you shouldn't assume everything with "natural"
on the label is guaranteed safe. Furthermore, some natural treatments that are harmless by themselves can cause

The chemicals found in the foxglove plant are used to make a powerful heart medication called Digitalis.

serious side effects when combined with other medications, which is why it's good to talk with a doctor even when taking nonprescription treatments.

I don't want to sound like a broken record, or like a know-it-all big sister, but . . . talk to Mom and see if she'll find a doctor who is open to alternative treatments for depression.

I'm really concerned, so write back soon!

—Linda

The Difficulty of Defining "Natural"

"Natural" treatments include just about anything except for "artificial/human-made drugs." Yet even that distinction is unclear: pharmacognosy, the study of natural drugs and their ingredients, sometimes leads to the development of prescription drugs produced by big pharmaceutical companies. If a medicine derived from an herb (a plant useful for medicine) is valuable enough, a drug company will apply for approval from the FDA to patent and market the drug. This process usually takes ten years and $200 million to accomplish, so it requires the efforts of a sizable company.

Of prescription drugs sold in the United States, one out of four contains phytochemicals, active healing ingredients obtained from plants. These plant-based medicines generate billions of dollars of sales every year in the United States. Most customers don't realize they are buying plant-based products because the botanical ingredients are listed by their chemical names, not the name of the plant from which they are

Drug Approval

Before a drug can be marketed in the United States, it must be officially approved by the Food and Drug Administration (FDA). Today's FDA is the primary consumer protection agency in the United States. Operating under the authority given it by the government and guided by laws established throughout the twentieth century, the FDA has established a rigorous drug approval process that verifies the safety, effectiveness, and accuracy of labeling for any drug marketed in the United States.

While the United States has the FDA for the approval and regulation of drugs and medical devices, Canada has a similar organization called the Therapeutic Product Directorate (TPD). The TPD is a division of Health Canada, the Canadian government department of health. The TPD regulates drugs, medical devises, disinfectants, and sanitizers with disinfectant claims. Some of the things that the TPD monitors are quality, effectiveness, and safety. Just as the FDA must approve new drugs in the United States, the TPD must approve new drugs in Canada before those drugs can enter the market.

derived. That's why the line between artificial, human made medicines and natural treatments can be somewhat blurry.

When people speak of natural treatments, however, they are usually *not* referring to medicines **patented**, tested, and produced by major pharmaceutical companies. One distinction between natural treatments and medicines produced by pharmaceutical companies is the complexity of chemical composition. FDA-approved commercial medicines usually are made of a limited number of isolated, purified chemicals. By contrast, natural treatments are usually made directly from one or more herbs, dried, crushed, and made into pills, powders, or other forms. Plants contain an astonishing number of various chemicals; most of them have never been completely analyzed in terms of their parts. Therefore, a product produced directly from an herb will have a much more complex chemical formula than a synthetically produced drug. Fans of

The peppermint plant has been used as a medicine since the 1700s. The modern medical world is also recognizing that this plant is good for more than just a flavoring; research indicates it is useful for treating intestinal conditions.

The thistle plant has been used as an herbal treatment
for liver disorders for more than two thousand
years. Over the past 40 years, intensive chemical,
pharmacological, and clinical research has confirmed
that thistle contains a chemical called silymarin,
which is useful for treating a variety of liver diseases.

natural treatments claim that this extra complexity can produce healing potential that is difficult to match artificially.

Let the Buyer Beware

The term "natural" in health treatments often refers to another factor, one that may be less positive for the buyer. Most of them are *not* FDA approved; this means they have not been through a scientific process of testing for safety and **efficacy** in healing illness. Because they have not been approved and licensed by the FDA, most natural or alternative treatments for depression are sold not as medicines but as "herbal dietary supplements." One person who has suffered from depression and posted his experiences on the Internet points out,

> This is a totally *unregulated* market, as opposed to traditional psychiatry, where psychiatric medications are subject to government approval, physicians and counselors are licensed, etc. Remember the saying *caveat emptor*, or "buyer beware." The claims made on bottles of St. John's Wort (for example) aren't required to be proven true. Practitioners of "holistic healing" (whatever that is—there isn't even a standard definition for it!) are not licensed or overseen. Be careful and aware of what you are getting into.

Homeopathy: An Alternative Medical System

According to the National Center for Homeopathy, "Homeopathy is a system of medicine that is based on the law of similars." It relies on a Latin phrase: *Similia Similibus Curentur*,

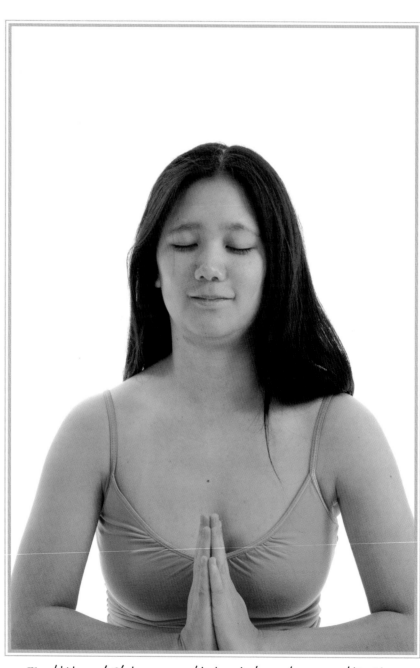

*Traditional Chinese medicine is based on meditation
and breathing, as well as the concepts of yin
and yang (negative and positive energies).*

utside of Science: Non-European raditions and Energy Therapies

2i gong is an ancient Chinese healing and well-being system using novement, meditation, relaxation, mind–body integration, and breathing xercises.

Reiki is a Japanese system of transferring energy from the practitioner o heal the patient. Reiki masters do not touch patients directly but ransfer healing power through the air.

Native American healing may include chants, drumming, burning sage, herbs, sweat lodges, dreams, and rituals to heal the patient's soul, body, nd mind. Some American Indians are displeased with New Agers selling heir traditions as cures.

Traditional Chinese medicine is based on the flow of vital energy (chi) hroughout the body, balancing yin and yang (negative and positive nergies), using herbs, nutrition, meditation, acupuncture, and exercise.

which translates: "Let likes cure likes." When someone is ill, homeopaths prescribe very tiny amounts of a substance known to produce symptoms similar to those produced by the illness. For example, if someone is nauseated, a homeopath would give the patient a tiny amount of medicine known to **induce** vomiting. According to its advocates, homeopathy differs from conventional medicine inasmuch as "homeopathy attempts to stimulate the body to recover itself."

Julian Winston, editor of *Homeopathy Today*, describes how a homeopathic doctor helped her take charge of her own health. She affirms, "I had found a system of medicine that was gentle, safe, and effective." However, many conventional medical professionals are less enthused.

In an article titled "Homeopathy: The Ultimate Fake," Dr. Stephen Barrett claims homeopathic drugs are so diluted that the original substance has been entirely removed from the medicine. Therefore, any results claimed for such medicines can only be the result of a placebo factor. (In experiments, a placebo is a neutral substance—such as a sugar pill—given to an experimental subject in place of actual medicine. In many cases, the patient's symptoms will go away and the patient will claim she is "cured"—but the cure takes place as a result of the power of the patient's mind.)

Medicine or Mysticism?

Homeopaths claim to be scientists; they say their treatments are based on proven physical principles. Other forms of the healing arts, however, claim to connect the realms of "spirit" and matter—and these claims are obviously incapable of scientific proof. Many of these approaches are far more ancient than conventional medicine, originating in the practices of medicine men and shamans. Ancient spiritual therapies incorporate the philosophical and spiritual beliefs of non-Western cultures. Energy therapies involve focused attention on the energy fields that are believed to surround and penetrate the body (though such energy fields are scientifically unproven).

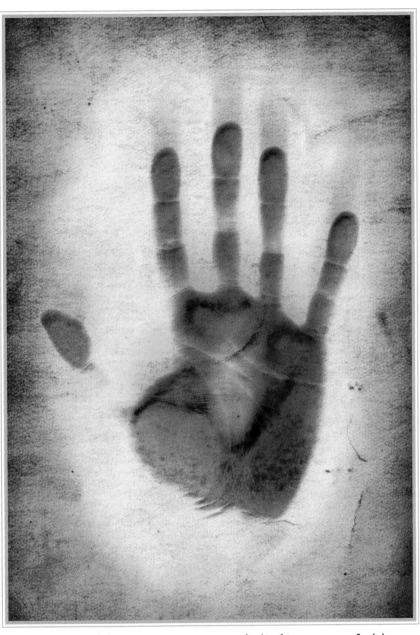

Some worldviews encompass a belief in energy fields that surround the human body. From this perspective emotional and physical healing is achieved through bringing these energies into balance.

Many Westerners have adopted Eastern medical practices. Some of these are reputable practitioners—and others aren't.

The decision whether these are actual cures or "hocus-pocus" depends largely on one's spiritual beliefs.

Traditional Doctors and Alternative Treatments

Doctors today are increasingly familiar with alternative treatments. If you are considering using natural treatments for depression, your doctor or psychiatrist may be able to tell you whether a particular approach is likely to be effective, and whether it can be used safely as a **complement** to conventional treatments. If you suffer from severe depression, you may be unwise to rely *solely* on alternative treatments; remember, they are legally unproven and results are uncertain. While some of the natural treatments have shown beneficial results in clinical tests, others have not, and some may have harmful side effects. Most important, keep hold of your common sense: if something seems too good to be true . . . it usually is.

Chapter 3

St. John's Wort: Big Claims for a Little Plant

Hi again Sis,

You'll be glad to know that I took your advice—and it turned out pretty good! I talked to Mom last week about how I've been feeling. I told her all the advice I've received from you and friends at school, and how I wanted to see a professional who was willing to look at alternative treatments for my depression. She really listened to me, then told me she was glad I talked to her. She got out the list of psychiatrists that our HMO will pay for and called several of them, asking if they were familiar with alternative treatments and willing to work with them. The third call, she found Dr. Graham, who seemed like just the doctor we were looking for.

Yesterday, I had my first meeting with Dr. Graham. She was really cool. She asked me a lot of questions about my life and how I've been feeling, and she listened to me explain how I'm concerned but confused about going on drugs as opposed to natural treatments. After all this, she suggested a variety of approaches to Mom and I that can help me feel better and best of all—she asked me if I felt comfortable with her suggestions. I do feel good about her ideas, especially since she treated me like part of the solution and not just the problem.

Anyway, Dr. Graham said I should go to a weekly meeting with something called a cognitive therapist, which is basically a talking cure for depression. She said a recent study shows cognitive therapy is as effective for treating depression as drugs are. She gave me the number for Dr. Susan Long, a therapist she recommends. Mom called her when we got home, and I won't be able to start seeing her until after Christmas, but that's okay—at least we have things started. Along with cognitive therapy, Dr. Graham suggested I try taking St. John's wort; she said it is often effective for many people with mildly to medium severe depression and it might work well together with the therapy. She also said she wants me to jog several miles, several times a week, because she doesn't think I'm getting enough exercise.

St. John's wort is a natural medication that
comes from a yellow-flowered plant.

St. John's wort

It sounds like a lot of work to get better, but I feel more hopeful now that things are happening. Thanks again for your advice; Mom and I are talking better than we were before, and I'm glad I found a professional who listens to me.

I can't wait to see you soon over Christmas break from your school.

—Krystal

Hi Krys,

I'm so glad you are getting help—and super-glad that your first visit with a professional turned out so good.

St. John's wort has really helped some people and I've heard good things about cognitive therapy too, so it sounds like a plan.

I'll see you at home soon. Send some good thoughts my way as I finish up my classes, I'm always sending mine your way.

—Linda

St. John's Wort: What Is It?

"Wort" sounds like something you would want removed if it grew on your nose, but don't confuse this word with wart. "Wort" is an old-fashioned word for "plant," and St. John's wort is a little plant that has generated much excitement over the years as a treatment for depression. The plant's scientific name is Hypericum perforatum, meaning "plant that grows under the heather." Since the days of the ancient Greeks, it

MIDSUMMER—THE BONFIRE.

St. John's Eve, also known as Midsummer's Eve and the Summer Solstice, is June 23. On that night, people would go into the woods and bring back branches to their homes, celebrating the eve of the birth of John the Baptist. Bonfires were built; fairies were said to speak in human tongues; and St. John's wort, the flower of happiness, bloomed. Flowers of St. John's wort were collected in Britain and Europe on St. John's Eve and worn on the body or hung over doorways as protection against witches. It was also brewed as a medicine to cure depression and madness.

has been used for a variety of medicinal uses. In recent years, it has been widely used and studied in the United States and Europe for treatment of depression.

Effectiveness for Treating Depression

More than a hundred clinical trials have been conducted on Hypericum in both the United States and Europe. In 2002, a French

Folktales

No one knows for sure how Hypericum came to be called St. John's wort. One guess is that it was so named since the plant flowers around June 23, the date of the Feast of Saint John in Christian tradition. One legend says that when Saint John was beheaded, the plant sprung up from his blood. Another possible reason for the name is that the Knights of Saint John of Jerusalem, a special order of Crusaders, used the herb for healing.

From ancient times through the medieval period, people believed St. John's wort had magical powers. During the Middle Ages, many people believed evil spirits caused depression, and Hypericum had magical powers to cast out these demons. The following is a medieval poem about St. John's wort:

St. John's wort doth charm all witches away
If gathered at midnight on the saint's holy day.
Any devils and witches have no power to harm
Those that gather the plant for a charm.

study using the most rigorous scientific methods, found Hypericum to be more effective than a placebo in treatment of mild to moderate depression. A German study the year prior found that Hypericum worked as effectively as fluoxetine (Prozac) for treatment of minor to moderate depression, with fewer side effects. The same year, another German study reported that Hypericum is a potentially safe and effective treatment for children with symptoms of depression with good *tolerability* and no adverse side effects. Yet another study, at the University of Vienna, reported "St. John's wort preparations have better safety and tolerability profiles than synthetic antidepressants." The summary of scientific trials is this: St. John's wort is effective for treatment of mild to moderate depression, with fewer side effects than those that accompany prescription antidepressants. These studies agree with the wort's long history of effective usage in treating depression.

A 2002 study was much quoted in the United States, however, as "bursting the bubble" on Hypericum. This experimental trial compared three different groups of patients with severe depression: some received Hypericum, others received a placebo, and a third group received sertraline (Zoloft), a commonly prescribed prescription antidepressant. The study concluded, "neither sertraline nor *H perforatum* was significantly different from placebo." In other words, St. John's wort may not help treat symptoms of major depression—but then a commonly used antidepressant drug may not work any better.

How does St. John's wort work to combat depression? Despite all the testing done on the plant, no one is sure. Some researchers believe that it affects the level of serotonin used to

*The scientific evidence on the efficacy of this little
yellow flower is still fairly inconclusive.*

communicate between neurons in the brain: Hypericum may work chemically in a way similar to synthetically produced SSRI medications like Prozac (fluoxetine) and Zoloft (sertraline).

Suggestions for Use

Even though most of the research is positive, keep in mind that Hypericum is *not* legally approved, patented, or regulated as a medicine by the FDA. Therefore, unlike legally marketed drugs, there is no official standard for dosage, degree of purity, or form of Hypericum that people use to treat depression. However, evidence from testing suggests the following as an ideal prescription for Hypericum in the treatment of depression: for adults with mild to moderate depression, take 300 mg of Hypericum in capsule form, three times a day (this fits conveniently with most people's morning, noon, and evening meal schedules).

Warnings and Cautions

Although Hypericum has been proven to compare favorably with prescription antidepressant medications, there are important factors to note regarding the safe use of this herb. First, *taking Hypericum alongside of prescription antidepressants may be dangerous.* A 2003 FDA warning stated, "Caution: many drugs interact with St. John's wort, including other antidepressants . . . oral contraceptives, antiretroviral, anti-cancer and anti-rejection drugs. Care should be taken to ask all patients what medications they are taking, including over-the-counter and supplements, to avoid these interactions." Furthermore, a 2006

Hypericum—St. John's wort—has never been approved by the FDA, which means that its purity and form may vary a great deal.

study by University of Virginia ***toxicologists*** reported that St. Johns wort is one of the most common herbal products reported to cause herb–drug interactions. Research also shows that St. John's wort may reduce the effectiveness of prescription drugs for heart disease, depression, seizures, or cancer. That's why it's always important to talk to a doctor before taking a natural remedy: remember the old saying, "He who treats himself has a fool for a doctor!"

Another reason why patients should talk with a doctor about their use of St. John's wort is this: it has been proven to be helpful with mild to moderate depression but not for treatment of major depression. How do you know if your depression is "moderate" or "severe"? You don't—which is why a professional doctor's opinion is so valuable.

Patients taking Hypericum for depression should also note that it doesn't begin working overnight. Typically, patients take about six weeks of regular treatment with Hypericum before noting any significant results. Many people begin taking the herb and then quit using it because "it isn't helping" before it has had time to work.

Side Effects

Hypericum has been used extensively for treatment of depression in Germany (sixty-six million daily doses in 1994), and this widespread use has not resulted in medical reports of serious harm caused by the herb. Hypericum is safer than aspirin: approximately five hundred people die every year from aspirin in the United States, but no deaths have yet been attributed to Hypericum. In massive doses Hypericum lessens

St. John's wort does not work immediately; it generally takes about six weeks before patients see any results.

*St. John's wort is just one of several
herbal remedies for depression.*

the resistance of skin to sunlight (a condition known as pho-totoxicity), but the effect is so slight no one has reported being harmed by it. Hypericum is so safe that in fifteen scientific studies, patients taking placebos reported more side effects than those taking Hypericum.

Still, there are no "perfect" medicines; Hypericum works reasonably well for milder cases of depression, but its uses are limited. Furthermore, it should not be used alongside other medications without the recommendation of a physician. And Hypericum is by no means the only herbal treatment for depression.

Chapter 4

Kava Kava and Other Natural Treatments

Hi again Sis,

*I*t was great having you home for a while, and thanks so much for letting me bend your ear over the holidays. I loved our trip to Rodeo Drive; it was just like old times.

Sorry to say, but I'm feeling pretty bad again. You know I never felt great over the past few weeks, but with you here and people to talk to it was better than it is now. Lately, I just wake up feeling lost, sad . . . and the whole

Kava kava grows wild in Hawaii and
other Polynesian islands.

day is pretty much the same. Today I was in the bathroom at school, crying, and a teacher's aide came in and found me. She wanted me to go see the nurse, but I told her that I already had seen a psychiatrist and I was getting help. She said "It doesn't seem to be helping much"—which got me thinking.

I did some more research online and noticed that kava root (they call it kava kava too) can be used to treat depression, and they claim it works right away. I'm wondering if I should switch to kava?

I just hate feeling this way all the time, I'm afraid my friends are all going to get sick of hanging around someone who is so down so often. I've been trying to jog, and I just hate it. I'm afraid this shrink that Dr. Graham set up is going to be awful. I just don't know what to do. Do you think kava kava might be the answer?

—Krystal

Hey Krys,
I'm sorry to hear how bad you are feeling again: wish I could be there to hug you and talk!

However, I'm not surprised that you're still struggling. Depression can last a long time so I didn't expect it to be all better overnight. St. John's wort can take up to several months before it becomes fully effective in your body, so don't stop taking that: just give it time to kick in.

Should you try kava kava? It might be a good idea, because as you said, it begins at once rather than the months

it takes St. John's wort to begin working. One caution, however: kava is effective for combating stress and anxiety, but
I'm not sure how much it would help with the sadness you
are experiencing. One big thing: too much kava can destroy
your liver—so you can't take large amounts for very long!

Why don't you call Dr. Graham and leave a message—
see what she thinks? Again, your doctor (not your big sister) knows best.

Hang in there; life will get better—but it is going to take
time.

—Linda

Joy Juice in Polynesian Paradise

Kava kava is a natural **tranquilizer**; its scientific name is
Piper methysticum, which means "intoxicating pepper." The
word *kava* is a Polynesian term meaning "bitter" or "sharp."
It grows throughout a number of beautiful South Pacific islands, including Hawaii, Papua New Guinea, Fiji, Samoa,
Vanuatu, and Tahiti. The kava plant is a leafy shrub with
many branches, growing to a height of eight feet. The plant's
healing properties reside in its roots, which are a large, tan-
gled mass.

Several different legends tell about the origins of the kava
plant. According to the Tonga Islands' mythology, someone
sacrificed the daughter of a chieftain at a time of great cri-
sis—and the plant grew from this daughter's remains. The
gods then showed the chief how to make a ceremonial drink
from the kava root.

Harvesting kava

In the 1700s, European explorers on the expedition led by Captain James Cook traveled to the Pacific Islands, where they first encountered kava. They reported that *indigenous* islanders held social gatherings around kava drink, which they served in a halved coconut shell. The drink was formed by chewing the roots of the kava plant. Polynesian islanders still prepare the kava drink by chewing, and they still hold

In the 1700s, when Captain Cook visited the Pacific Islands, he was honored with a kava ceremony.

kava ceremonies for important visiting guests. Former president Lyndon Johnson, Pope John Paul II, Hillary Clinton, and Queen Elizabeth have all been greeted with kava.

In the Polynesian Islands, kava kava was (and is) prized for its effects. After imbibing kava drink, islanders became more sociable and relaxed. Unlike alcohol, kava relaxes without impairing the senses; kava users report being more "in the moment" and focused when under the root's influence. The most important effect noted by kava users is relief from stressed or anxious feelings; situations that would otherwise cast them into panic or sink them into depression do not affect people taking kava.

The primary active ingredient in kava is called kavalactone and found only in the roots. For over a century, scientists have studied this substance to see how it works, but they haven't

No Hate with Kava Kava

Tom Harrison, in his book Savage Civilization *(1937), reported that when using kava kava, "Your head is affected most pleasantly. Thoughts come cleanly. You feel friendly . . . never cross. . . . You cannot hate with kava in you." No wonder kava has traditionally been used in Polynesian cultures for healing ceremonies—both inner healing and healing of interpersonal relationships.*

reached any definite conclusions. Extracts of kavalactone separated from the root don't work as effectively as medicines manufactured from ground-up portions of the whole root, so it seems that the plant's healing properties are the result of the complex formula of chemicals found in the whole plant.

Effective for Treating Anxiety

At least three dozen scientific tests of *Piper methysticum* have verified the root's tranquilizing properties. Kava outperforms placebos in terms of reducing low-level stress and generalized anxiety, anxiety associated with depression, and anxiety caused by ***menopause***. However, while it may help people get over a brief feeling of the blues caused by everyday stress, kava is not necessarily helpful with clinical depression. A 2003 FDA report noted kava has "not been proven effective for the treatment of depression."

Suggested Use

As with all herbal dietary remedies, the FDA does not recognize kava kava as a medicine, and therefore, legal standards do not regulate the purity, dosage, or method of taking the root. Natural health practitioners recommend that kava be taken in 250-milligram doses, two or three times a day. *It should only be used intermittently, for no longer than one month, due to the possibility of permanent liver damage.*

Warnings and Side Effects

Enthusiasm over kava's stress-reducing potential has been considerably dampened by cases of liver damage. In Germany, more than forty cases of liver damage and several deaths have been linked to the root: therefore, Canada, Singapore, and Germany have banned kava products. In the United States, the FDA has issued warnings of possible liver damage, while conducting further research into possible dangers of kava products.

Polynesians prepare kava drink by chewing the roots of the kava plant.

If you are thinking of using kava kava, remember that taking it in high dosages or for any prolonged period may permanently ruin your liver, so kava should be used only sparingly. Avoid use of kava altogether if you consume alcohol, as the combination of kava and alcoholic beverages can hasten dam-

A modern-day visitor to the Pacific Islands enjoys the chance to experience kava.

age to the liver. Always tell your doctor you are taking kava before using any other medications.

SAM-e

Actually, SAM-e is not an herb, hormone, vitamin, or any other kind of nutrient; in fact, SAM-e (S-adenosylmethionine) is a synthetic form of a chemical produced naturally in the body. The fact that SAM-e is marketed as a natural alternative for depression is a little ironic: it is only "natural" in the sense that it is *unregulated* and can therefore be sold over the counter. In Europe, SAM-e is sold as a prescription drug, and most health experts agree that it should be tested and regulated in Canada and the United States as well.

There have been more than a dozen scientific tests of SAM-e's effectiveness in treating depression; together, these studies show SAM-e is superior to placebo and comparable to prescription antidepressants for treatment of patients with major depression. Side effects include mild insomnia, lack of appetite, constipation, nausea, dry mouth, diaphoresis, dizziness, and nervousness. Keep in mind that SAM-e has not been studied very much, so no one knows what long-term effects there might be and how it might interact with other drugs. Tests show it may worsen cases of **bipolar mood disorder** (manic-depressive illness). Although tests do show SAM-e is effective in addressing symptoms of depression, those taking it must remember that it is a synthetic chemical, largely unknown; users are basically guinea pigs in their own private, uncontrolled experiment.

5-HTP

5-HTP is short for L-5-hydroxytryptophan, a specific form of tryptophan, an amino acid that helps control the brain's production of serotonin. Tryptophan is the amino acid that naturally is found in turkey; it is the substance that makes you sleepy after a big Thanksgiving meal. Studies have shown 5-HTP is as effective as prescription antidepressants in treating depression. It is sold as an herbal dietary supplement, not requiring a prescription and legally unregulated in the United States—but like SAM-e it does not come from a plant or other natural substance.

5-HTP, short for L-5-hydroxytryptophan, is a serotonin precursor; in other words, its presence helps in the production of this neurotransmitter.

Side effects or risks possibly associated with 5-HTP are still unknown, but medical scientists urge caution in using it because of problems related to tryptophan in general. Thirty-seven people died and more than a thousand were permanently damaged by tryptophan in the late 1980s when they contracted a disease called EMS (eosinophilia myalgia syndrome), resulting in paralysis and other dire effects. Most if not all the cases of EMS were connected with tryptophan produced by one company, and advocates of 5-HTP blame the cases on contamination of the specific product rather than tryptophan itself. Nonetheless, doctors recommend eating turkey as a safer way to get relaxing amino acids until more research is conducted on 5-HTP.

Omega-3 Fatty Acids

Omega-3 fatty acids play a role in the function of **neurotransmitters** in the human nervous system and hence affect moods. These acids can be found in flax seed, soybeans, avocados, tofu, and fish. They are also sold as dietary supplements in pharmacies and health-food stores. Recent scientific tests show that omega-3 fatty acids added onto existing treatments helped with the irritability component of a significant percentage of patients suffering from bipolar disorder, a finding that reinforces previous research showing the helpfulness of omega-3 fatty acids for treatment of depression. Physicians recommend an increased dietary intake of omega-3 fatty acids, either through food, fish oil, or capsules, as complementary treatment alongside other prescribed medications for treating depression. The same acids have been shown to reduce risk of heart attack, so it wouldn't hurt for everyone to increase their intake of foods rich in this substance. Intense research is being devoted to these substances and their beneficial effects on the body.

Ginkgo Biloba

Ginkgo biloba is a tree whose leaves have been used for over five thousand years as an herbal medicine in China. Research has focused on its use as treatment for patients suffering from Alzheimer's disease, *dementia*, and other illnesses characterized by loss of brain functions; results are promising for gingko as treatment for these conditions. Some tests indicate that gingko lessens depression related to memory loss, dementia, or other memory-related illnesses. Physicians suggest that it should not be used as a primary treatment for most patients with major depression, but should be considered for elderly patients with depression resistant to standard drug therapy. So far, tests have revealed few side effects. It is unknown how gingko interacts with prescription antidepressants.

B Vitamins

Evidence indicates that moderate depression may be caused by lack of certain vitamins, especially B6 and B12. These vitamins play a role in the health of the brain's neurotransmitters. Taking mass quantities of Vitamin B will not treat most cases of depression, and doing so may empty a patient's pocketbook; however, anyone suffering from depression should make sure he or she is getting a recommended daily dose of

The ginkgo is an ancient tree that has been
used as an herbal medicine in China for
more than five thousand years.

Research indicates that ginkgo may be a good treatment for elderly people with depression and memory loss.

vitamins B6 and B12—1.3 milligrams for males and 1.7 milligrams for females.

A number of nonprescription substances may help alleviate mild to moderate depression, or specific symptoms related to depression. At the same time, some of these may have harmful side effects, and many of them are poorly researched. Always work closely with a licensed physician when considering dietary supplements as a primary treatment or complementary treatment for depression.

Some natural treatments, however, don't have to be eaten, taken as a drink, or as pills. Many experts believe the best treatment for depression is the talking cure. What could be more natural than talking?

Chapter 5

Talking Cures

Hi again Sis,

Thanks for the encouragement in your last e-mail; I know I need to keep on fighting this depression, and I don't really expect it to go away overnight. It's just hard keeping up with everything the doctor said to do when I don't see results yet.

Anyway, yesterday was a new adventure in my ongoing battle against unhappiness. I had my first appointment with Dr. Long, the psychologist Dr. Graham recommended. I guess I had some funny ideas of what a psychologist would look like—I was expecting a female version of Sigmund Freud, with a funny German accent, dressed in stuffy

Some psychiatrists may prescribe drug treatment while they also offer psychotherapy; others, however, may refer patients to another therapist for counseling.

Victorian garb. However, Dr. Long wasn't what I was expecting! She's pretty young, has great taste in fashion, and was real easy to talk to.

She explained that our first session was mostly getting to know me, and she would focus more directly on my depression in later sessions. She said we would talk about how my thoughts, feelings, and events in my life connect to each other. She said sometimes talk therapy can be difficult—I may need to share things that are hard to talk about, and I might learn things about myself that I have avoided in the past. If someone at school said stuff like that I'd freak, but Dr. Long seems really cool, so I'm okay. She seems really caring and intelligent, so maybe she is part of the answer for all this. Like Dr. Graham, she told me that getting on top of this depression is going to be a combination of things; talking with her, sticking with the St. John's wort and—yuck—jogging.

Anyway, I still feel sad a lot, but yesterday made me hopeful about the future again. I'm actually looking forward to meeting next week with Dr. Long. I think she can really help me.

—Krystal

Hiya Krys,

I'm glad to hear your visits with Dr. Long are a success. She doesn't sound anything like old Dr. Freud, but watch out if she starts asking you about your potty training (LOL).

Say "hi" to Mom. I need to call and chat with her some-time soon. Oh, and everyone on the floor loved those cook-ies you sent—I hardly got to eat any myself! Any chance you can send more?

Keep me posted on everything. And again, hang in there. I know this darkness in your life is going to lift—it just takes time and effort.

Love you!

—Linda

Cognitive Therapy

Cognitive therapy is sometimes called thought therapy; it's a form of psychotherapy, or talking cure. Of all the so-called natural cures, this one is the best-researched approach to treatment of depression. Cognitive therapy works by helping the patient understand and change her thought patterns to improve feelings.

You may think you are very aware of your feelings; after all, we live inside our heads 24/7, so how can we *not* be aware of our emotions? Yet surprisingly, many people have little real awareness of their feelings; it is often easier to ignore them or deliberately misunderstand them. One therapist compares feelings to the "check engine" light on a car's dashboard; many people prefer to keep on driving rather than look under the hood for fear of what they might find there.

Certain thoughts lead to depressed feelings, and these thoughts are most often distorted. Depressed patients often ex-aggerate how bad things are, or they have a narrow, restricted

Our thoughts shape our emotions.

If you tell yourself you will always be unhappy, chances are you may be.

focus on dismal facts. A cognitive therapist can help his client realize when he is distorting his thinking and consequently replace these depression-causing thoughts with more helpful thinking.

For example, a depressed person often believes the reason for her unhappiness is inside herself. For example, she might think, "No one likes me because I am ugly and stupid," She may also believe her unhappiness is permanent. She might think, "I will always be unhappy. No one will ever like me." She also tends to believe that she is helpless: "there is nothing I can do to change my life." A cognitive therapist will teach her to replace this negative "self-talk" with more positive thought habits. For instance, the depressed person can practice telling herself these thoughts instead: "People in this school are so focused on themselves and their schoolwork, it's no wonder

Depression as Opportunity

Most people think of depression as completely negative, and that makes perfect sense, given how awful one feels struggling with feelings of sadness and despair. However, Dr. Frederic Flach, in his book The Secret Strength of Depression, *suggests another perspective. He writes, "To experience acute depression is an opportunity for us not just to learn more about ourselves, but to become more whole."*

I'm having a hard time getting to know them better." "I'm going through a rough time right now, but soon things will be better." "It may take me some time, but I can learn how to get along in this situation."

Effectiveness

Research shows that cognitive therapy is as effective as antidepressant medications in treating depression; furthermore, it has even been shown to have positive effects in altering brain

Talking with someone who can help you look at your thought habits has proved to be one of the most effective treatments for battling depression.

chemistry. An article in the January 2006 *American Family Physician* reported:

> Numerous studies . . . demonstrate convincingly that cognitive therapy or CBT effectively treats patients with unipolar major depression. . . . They also showed that cognitive therapy is as effective and possibly more effective than pharmacotherapy in managing mild to moderate unipolar depression.

The same article recommends, "CBT should be strongly considered as initial therapy for patients with severe or chronic depression or for adolescents."

Cognitive therapy is an effective and widely used nonmedicinal treatment for depression. However, there are other nonmedicinal forms of treatment for depression: some of these are common-sense practices, while others are less traditional non-Western practices.

Chapter 6

A Holistic Health Approach

Hi Sis,

I figured after all the depressed e-mails I've sent over the past few months, you'd be glad to get some good news, so here it is: I'm feeling much better these days! It didn't happen all at once like some great miracle. I can't point to a certain day or week when things changed, but I for sure am in a different place. I wake up in the morning looking forward to the day—what a change that is! I've started playing b-ball after school again, and I'm staying active in the evening too, so I can hang out more with friends.

Months ago, when Dr. Graham suggested everything she wanted me to do, I thought, "This is gonna be a pain in the butt—take St. John's wort, see a psychologist, and jog—how can I do all this stuff?" Now, I wonder how I survived without these practices. It's not like I'm just taking medicine, more like I've learned how to have a whole life. I mean, there's something about the discipline of it all that's really good for me. I used to hate exercising, but now I run a few miles every morning, and if I don't run, I really miss it. Who would ever have imagined?

Regular aerobic exercise can improve a person's mood.

Dr. Long said last meeting that I was doing much better and maybe I could stop seeing her. I told her how much I would miss our weekly sessions. She really has been great!

Last year my depression was awful, but today, I feel like myself again. I have a life, and I am so thankful to everyone who helped, especially you, Sis. I thank God for my big sister. What would I have done without you?

—Krystal

Hey Krys,

You go, girl—and don't forget to give yourself some credit; you made important decisions and got the help you needed. You're the one living a healthy life every day. I'm so proud of you and happy for you. You rock!

—Linda

Depression and Exercise

There is one treatment for depression that can be almost 100 percent free, totally natural, and almost completely safe—physical exercise!

Depression is a complicated illness caused by multiple factors such as genes, family background, choices and events in life, brain chemicals, thought patterns, general physical health, and personality. Such a complex illness is unlikely to be treated effectively by just one approach. Research suggests regular exercise may be an effective way to complement other treatments and lift a person's mood.

Studies in the United States and England indicate that a regular exercise program can yield results similar to drug treatment of depression, and a combination of chemical treatment with physical exercise is even more effective. Serotonin is important for the performance of neurotransmitters in the human body, and ***aerobic exercise*** helps increase production of serotonin. Furthermore, aerobic exercise helps strengthen the heart, lungs, blood vessels—one's whole body benefits from physical fitness. Since depression involves the whole body, a person can fight against depression more effectively when his entire body is fit.

A healthy diet, based on this diagram, can contribute to healthier emotions as well as a healthier body.

You Are What You Eat

Depression sometimes causes decreased appetite and weight loss; it may also cause food cravings and weight gain. Either way, someone who is depressed becomes less healthy due to changes in food intake. As the body's intake of nutrients changes, depression is likely to become worse. So when someone is depressed, a healthy, balanced diet is especially important. Persons struggling with depression should strive to do the following:

• Eat sensible, well-balanced meals.

• Don't skip meals.

• Drink alcohol only in very small amounts or not at all.

• Don't be hard on yourself if you eat an occasional chocolate chip cookie (chocolate can be therapeutic—but see the next item) .

• Avoid eating too many simple carbohydrates (white rice, bagels, cookies, crackers, beer, wine, and pastas), as these cause moods to briefly lift but then fall.

• Strive instead to eat complex carbohydrates (whole grains, beans, vegetables and whole fruits) that help moods to stabilize.

Yoga is an effective antidepressant treatment.

Why isn't exercise more publicized as treatment for depression? Partly because the nature of depression itself makes regular exercise difficult. Depression slows down the body; deeply depressed patients don't even want to get out of bed, let alone take a jog around the block! Physical exercise is good medicine for depression, but it can also be a bitter medicine. For this reason, it may be helpful for a person who is depressed to have friends or family who encourage him to get out and do something physical, even if he is reluctant to do so. Some individuals may need treatment for depression before they can find enough energy to take on an exercise routine.

Yoga

Yoga is an ancient health practice originating in India; it involves slow stretching, balancing, and breathing exercises believed to increase overall well-being. A couple of studies have investigated the effects of yoga exercises on depression. One study showed that practicing yoga produced faster improvement than no treatment did. The other study found yoga was as effective as an antidepressant drug for patients with major depression, but less effective than ***electroconvulsive therapy***.

Shed Some Light on the Situation

People who experience depression particularly during long, dark winter months may suffer from a specific form of depression called seasonal affective disorder (SAD). SAD may be treated similarly to other forms of depression, but one of

Spirituality contributes to mental health.

the most popular treatments is light therapy. Light therapy involves artificial lighting ranging from twenty-five to a hundred times more powerful than a standard hundred-watt lightbulb. Exposure to this bright light usually lasts from a half hour to two hours daily. A simpler alternative is to walk outdoors during the brightest daylight (though this does not help much in areas that are consistently overcast). Studies on this form of therapy are inconclusive: some research suggests it is no more effective than taking a placebo—yet many people say light therapy has helped them significantly.

Mindfulness and Spirituality

Professor Mark Williams, of the Department of Psychology at the University of Wales, studied the effects of meditation on depression. Subjects were told to practice mindfulness by focusing on a single physical object. In the year following the test, those patients who received meditation training suffered only half as much depression as those without meditation.

Psychiatrist Richard Flach, author of *The Secret Strength of Depression*, cites studies that "indicate that people who are more religiously active have fewer depressive symptoms" than those without such spiritual beliefs. Dr. Flach emphasizes that religiosity is by no means insurance against depression, but "religious coping . . . appears to mitigate . . . symptoms of depression." So for persons inclined toward religious belief, continuing to practice customary spiritual rituals may help combat depression.

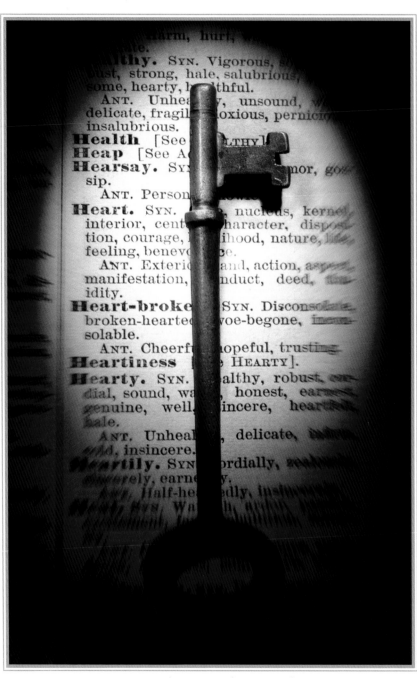

*There may be more than one key to
emotional and physical health.*

A Final Reminder

There are a host of alternative treatments for depression, varying in effectiveness. Doctors today are increasingly open to alternative treatments. If you suffer from depression, it is always best to discuss your symptoms with a health-care professional.

Further Reading

Bratman, Steven. *Beat Depression with St. John's Wort*. New York: Prima, 2001.

Cobain, Bev. *When Nothing Matters Anymore: A Survival Guide for Depressed Teens*. Minneapolis, Minn.: Free Spirit, 2002.

Elliot, Charles H., and Laura L. Smith. *Depression for Dummies*. Indianapolis, Ind.: Wiley, 2003.

Flach, Frederic. *The Secret Strength of Depression: Third Revised Edition*. New York: Hatherleigh Press, 2002.

Johnsgard, Keith. *Conquering Depression & Anxiety Through Exercise*. New York: Prometheus, 2004.

Knishinsky, Ran. *The Prozac Alternative: Natural Relief from Depression with St. John's Wort, Kava, Ginkgo, 5-HTP, Homeopathy, and Other Alternative Remedies*. Rochester, Vt.: Healing Arts Press, 2000.

Mindell, Earl. *All About Kava*. New York: Avery, 2005.

Thase, Michael E., and Susan S. Lang. *Beating the Blues: New Approaches to Overcoming Dysthymia and Chronic Mild Depression*. New York: Oxford University Press, 2004.

For More Information

CNN.com: Health
www.cnn.com/HEALTH

Depression-guide.com: Alternative Treatments
www.depression-guide.com/alternative-treatment-depression.htm

HealthyPlace.com: Depression Community
www.healthyplace.com/Communities/Depression/treatment/antidepressants/index.asp

HerbMed
www.herbmed.org

Hypericum.Com: St. John's Wort & Depression Homepage
www.hypericum.com

Kava
www.geocities.com/chadrx/kava.html

KavaRoot.com
www.kavaroot.com

Natural Antidepressant News & Views
www.mts.net/~baumel/News&Views.html

Psychiatric Times
www.psychiatrictimes.com

Glossary

aerobic exercise: Physical activity that increases respiration and heart rates.

bipolar mood disorder: A psychological condition characterized by extreme highs alternating with extreme lows.

cognitive: Relating to the process of acquiring knowledge.

complement: Something that completes or enhances something else.

dementia: A deterioration of intellectual functions that can occur while other brain functions remain intact.

diaphoresis: Sweating caused by medical conditions.

efficacy: The ability to produce the desired results.

electroconvulsive therapy: The passing of a small electric current through the brain to induce a seizure, used in the treatment of severe psychiatric disorders.

homeopathy: A treatment method in which the patient is given minute doses of natural drugs that in larger doses would produce symptoms of the disease itself.

indigenous: Native to an area.

induce: Bring about, cause.

menopause: The time in a woman's life when menstruation ceases.

neurobiological: Relating to the scientific study of the molecular and cellular levels of the nervous system, of systems within the brain such as vision and hearing, and behavior produced by the brain.

neurons: Cells that transmit nerve impulses and are the basic functional unit of the nervous system.

neurotransmitters: Chemicals that carry messages between different nerve cells and muscles.

patented: Granted the exclusive right to make or sell an invention.

psychosocial: Relating to both the psychological and the social aspects of something.

Qi gong: An ancient Chinese system using movement, meditation, relaxation, mind–body integration, and breathing exercises in the treatment of illness.

Reiki: A Japanese system of treating illness using the transfer of energy from the practitioner to the patient.

tolerability: The degree that something is not too unpleasant or severe to put up with.

toxicologists: Scientists trained to examine the adverse effects of chemicals on living organisms.

tranquilizer: A medication that reduces anxiety and tension.

Bibliography

American Family Physician: Cognitive Therapy for Depression. http://www.aafp.org/afp/20060101/83.html.

Better Health Channel: Depression and Exercise. http://www.betterhealth.vic.gov.au/bhcv2/bhcArticles.nsf/pages/Depression_and_exercise?OpenDocument.

Depression-guide.com: Alternative Treatments. http://www.depression-guide.com/alternative-treatment-depression.htm.

Dudley, William, ed. *The History of Drugs: Antidepressants.* Farmington Hills, Mich.: Greenhaven, 2005.

Elliot, Charles H., and Laura L. Smith. *Depression for Dummies*. Indianapolis: Wiley, 2003.

Flach, Frederic. *The Secret Strength of Depression: Third Revised Edition*. New York: Hatherleigh Press, 2002.

HealthyPlace.com: Natural Treatments for Depression. http://www.healthyplace.com/Communities/Depression/site/transcripts/natural_depression_treatments.asp.

Helpguide: Complementary and Alternative Approaches to Mental Health Treatment. http://www.helpguide.org/mental/complementary_alternative_mental_health_treatment.htm.

HerbMed. http://www.herbmed.org/index.asp.

Hypericum.Com: St. John's Wort & Depression Homepage. http://www.hypericum.com.

National Center for Homeopathy. http://www.homeopathic. org/index.html.

Nutrition Journal: Omega-3 fatty acids decreased irritability of patients with bipolar disorder in an add-on, open label study. http://www.nutritionj.com/content/4/1/6.

Quackwatch: Homeopathy. http://www.quackwatch.org/ 01QuackeryRelatedTopics/homeo.html.

Index

Picture Credits

Biographies

Author

Kenneth McIntosh is a freelance writer and teacher living in northern Arizona. He has written two dozen educational books, and taught at junior high, high school, and community college levels.

Consultant

Andrew M. Kleiman, M.D., received a Bachelor of Arts degree in philosophy from the University of Michigan, and earned his medical degree from Tulane University School of Medicine. Dr. Kleiman completed his internship, residency in psychiatry, and fellowship in forensic psychiatry at New York University and Bellevue Hospital. He is currently in private practice in Manhattan, specializing in psychopharmacology, psychotherapy, and forensic psychiatry. He also teaches clinical psychology at the New York University School of Medicine.